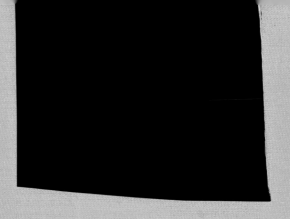

To Joe,
who always believes in me
—A. E. S.

•

For my sister Keri
—K. F.

•

For my mom,
who would've loved this
—K. D.

•

In loving memory
of my very good friend Bobdog
—S. K.

•

For Lila June and Harold
—C. McQ.

Amy E. Sklansky

From the Doghouse

Poems
to
Chew On

ILLUSTRATED BY

Karla Firehammer, Karen Dismukes,
Sandy Koeser, AND Cathy McQuitty

HENRY HOLT AND COMPANY · NEW YORK

Contents

Guess Who?

I've got four legs,
   and my paws are tough.

Two perky ears,
   and a voice that's gruff.

My coat is furry,
   and my nose is wet.

Here's a big hint:
   I'm your favorite pet!

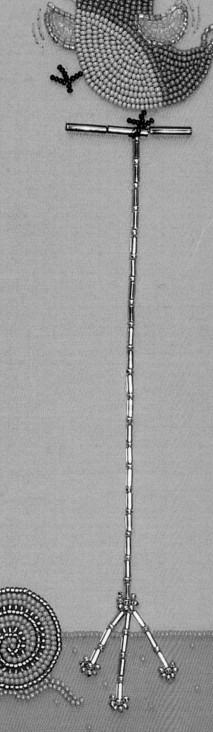

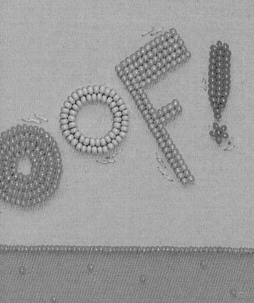

Important Instructions for My Master

If you can learn this one thing,
we'll get along just fine.

When you see me standing here
and I start to whine,

Please take me out
to lift my leg
and sniff the evening air.

Are you listening?
Fair warning.
Ignore me . . . if you dare.

Into Your Loving Arms I Leap

Into your loving arms I leap—
Please scratch between my ears.
I love the way you cuddle me
And ease my doggy fears.

Doggy Days

I greet Monday with a wag
  and Tuesday with a bark.

Wednesday gets a wiggle
  while I'm walking to the park.

I scratch to start a Thursday;
  on Friday I just stretch.

Saturday's my favorite
  'cause there's lots of time for fetch.

When Sunday comes I'm tired,
  so I curl up on the floor—

And dream my doggy dreams
  'til the week begins once more.

zZzZzZz

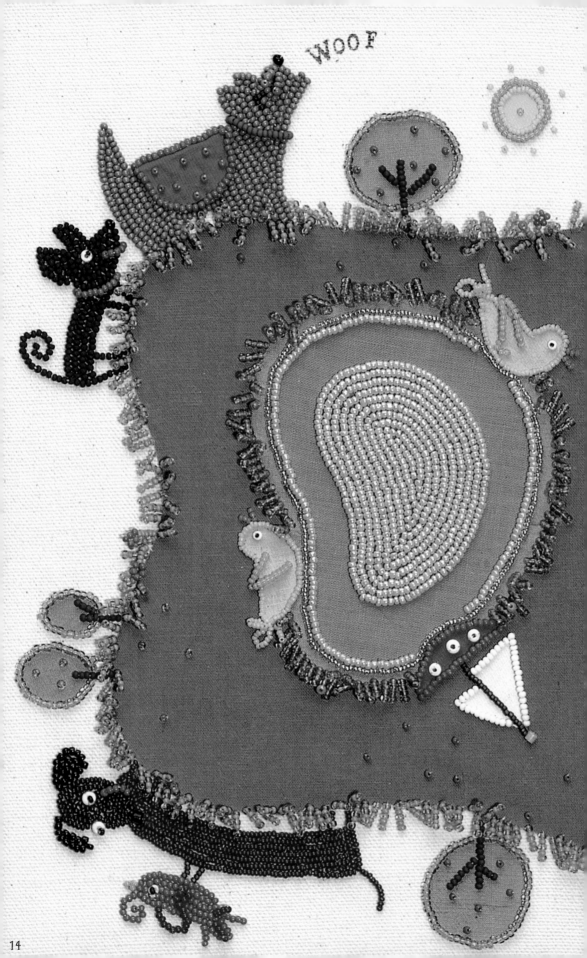

WOOF

14

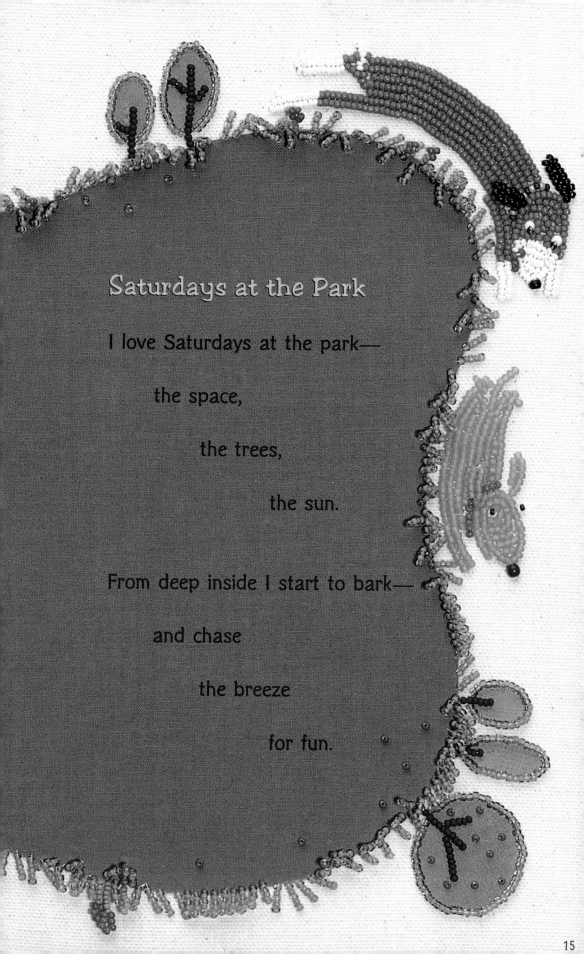

Saturdays at the Park

I love Saturdays at the park—

the space,

the trees,

the sun.

From deep inside I start to bark—

and chase

the breeze

for fun.

Rainy Day Dream

"It's raining cats and dogs!"
I thought I heard them say.

Whatever could they mean
on such a dismal day?

All I see are raindrops
and mud puddles galore.

How I wish it would rain cats
outside my doggy door.

Mud

Mud.   Mud.
   Muddy, muddy mud.

I roll over over and over and over,
   'til I'm covered
      in oozing, sucking,
         slippery, mucking
        mud.

Doggy Nightmare

I opened up my mouth to bark—
but out came a meow!

I tried to bark another time,
but there was no bow-wow.

Even with a bone to chew
I hankered after fish.

Maybe catnip would be nice
in a pretty kitty dish?

I thought, "Could I be crazy?"
as I lapped a bowl of cream.

Thank goodness I awoke
from that scary kitty dream.

I barked, and then I barked some more.
Hooray, it's really true!

I'm no silly kitty.
I'm a doggy's dog—that's who!

In Our Car

Sunlight warms my face.
Down the road we race.
  Zoom zoom zoom . . .

Ears flap in the breeze.
Zipping by the trees.
  Zoom zoom zoom . . .

Wind's the loudest sound.
Cruising over ground.
Zoom zoom zoom . . .

Home again so soon?
Let's ride tomorrow afternoon.
Zoom zoom zoom . . .

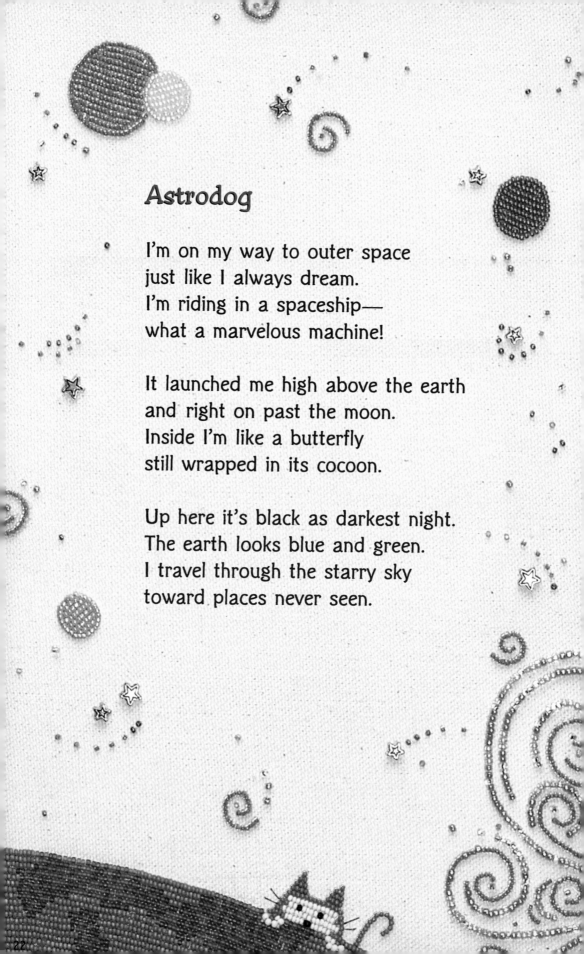

Astrodog

I'm on my way to outer space
just like I always dream.
I'm riding in a spaceship—
what a marvelous machine!

It launched me high above the earth
and right on past the moon.
Inside I'm like a butterfly
still wrapped in its cocoon.

Up here it's black as darkest night.
The earth looks blue and green.
I travel through the starry sky
toward places never seen.

23

Fetch

It's the ball.   The ball.
That good old tennis ball!

                                              I chase it down.

I bring it back.

                                    Chase it down.

         Bring it back.

                            Down.

              Back.

                    The ball.
                    The ball.
                    Throw the ball and I'll . . .

FETCH!

Digging

A sunny day,
the smell of grass,
and dirt beneath my paws—

    I think I'll dig
    a hole today.
    Why dig? Well, just because . . .

Because with luck
I just might find
an old forgotten bone.

    Or then again
    I just might find
    a treasure yet unknown.

Doggy Dream

Under a dark and moonlit sky,
night rushes past my face.
Don't wake me from this doggy dream
with all these stars to chase.

I hear the heavens call to me.
The wind begins to roar.
I stretch my wings and start to move—

I leap. I fly. I soar.

Round and Round

My tail won't stop its wagging.
My rear end has an ache.
Back and forth and back and forth—
it never takes a break!

Round and round in circles
I try to catch my tail.
But no matter what I do
I always seem to fail.

Still, I give it one more shot
and run with all my might.
I'm on the trail, I'm closing in—
but then it's out of sight.

One day I'll catch my furry tail.
For now, I'm just plain spent.
Where did that tail run off to?
Do *you* know where it went?

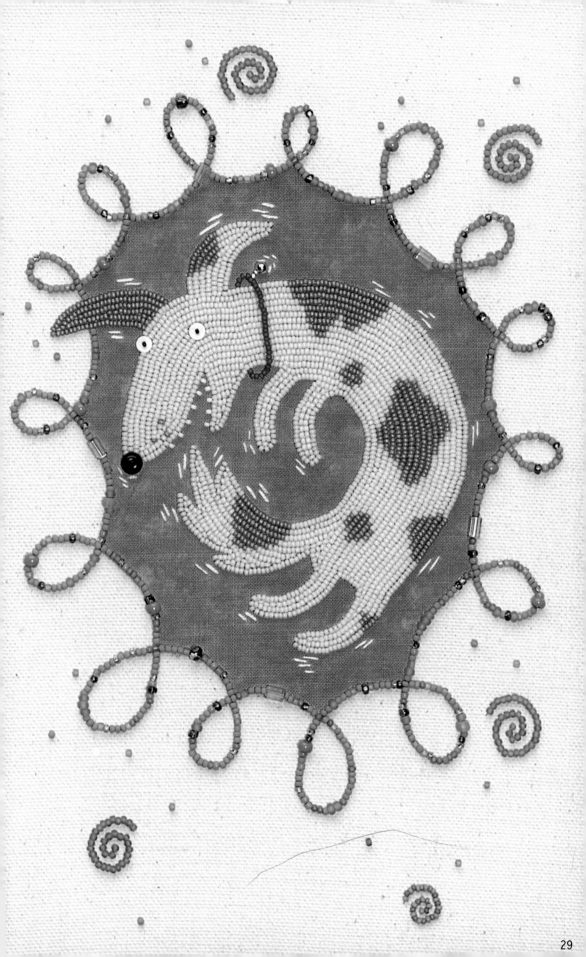

Old Friend

Red and standing tall—
Guardian of our block.

My Beloved Bone

Gnawed, savored, buried—
A present from the butcher.

Swimming

I don't do the backstroke
Or swim the butterfly.
Doggy paddle is my stroke—
I'll bet you can guess why!

Scuba Dogs

I saw some doggies dressing
in fins and scuba gear.
They dove into the ocean,
then quickly disappeared.

Did they dance with mermaids?
What wonders could there be
    deep
        deep
           d
                o
                   w
                     n

beneath the dark green sea?

Pesky Fleas

Oh, woe
is me,
these pesky fleas.

Too small
to see,
these pesky fleas.

They jump
and bite
all day
and night.
And so,
with all
my doggy might
I . . .

SCRATCH!

The Bath

splash
soap
scrub
mope

rinse
quake
dry
shake

mud
run
roll
done!

City Dog / Country Dog

"A hydrant," said the City Dog,
"is where I like to pee."
      "A hydrant?" asked the Country Dog.
      "I prefer a tree."

"I take a yellow taxicab
when I go downtown."
      "I ride in a pick-up truck
      with the window down."

"The park is where I like to run
and do my clever tricks."
   "The backyard is my favorite place
   to fetch and bury sticks."

"What makes me truly happy
is a big old juicy bone."
   "A juicy bone, my city friend?
   On that, you're not alone!"

Sheriff Doggy

I dreamt I was the sheriff
of a one-horse doggy town.
I brought the thieves to justice
and turned that town around.

When danger called, I answered
(with a badge upon my chest),
"Pups and dogs, you're safe with me:
This sheriff never rests."

At the Dog Show

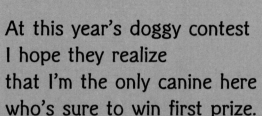

At this year's doggy contest
I hope they realize
that I'm the only canine here
who's sure to win first prize.

Bright pink bows perch on my ears,
my teeth gleam when I smile.
With this shiny coat of fur,
I'll beat them by a mile.

All attention's on the ring.
I do my snappy tricks:
Heel and sit and roll and shake,
then fancy backward flips.

When all the votes are counted
I've won the "Best in Show."
My fans all cheer and clap for me—
the cutest dog they know!

Nuzzle My Muzzle

Nuzzle my muzzle.
Fondle my fur.
Tickle my tummy.
And then . . .
   do it
   all over
   again!

By Name

Doggy
Puppy
Cur or Mutt.

Canine
Poochie
Hound or Pup.

No matter what we're called by name,
At heart we're doggies all the same.

Meet the Beaders

On a Saturday morning, you might find Karla Firehammer, Karen Dismukes, Sandy Koeser, and Cathy McQuitty at a "Bead 'n' Feed." After breakfast, they spend the morning beading together. Beading sessions can get a little hectic since they involve thousands of beads and often the most curious of their collective eight dogs and three cats.

The Beading Facts

• A single illustration can incorporate between 3,000 and 8,000 beads, as well as several kinds of fabric. It took about 120,000 beads to illustrate this book!

• The artists find beads everywhere: from garage sales to beading conventions, from Venice to Kansas City. Sometimes they even swap beads. They each have hundreds of containers of beads in a rainbow of colors.

• Beads are sewn onto canvas with a special thin thread that looks like dental floss.

• One illustration may require 40 to 120 hours of work, depending on the size of the piece and the number and type of beads.

When they're not beading or working . . .

 Karla walks her three dogs. (Her crabby cat stays at home.) Look for her dog Gatsby in "Sheriff Doggy."

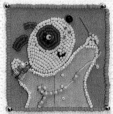 Sandy cans vegetables she's grown in her garden. Look for her dalmatian Bobdog on the Contents page.

 Karen loves to travel and once beaded while sitting on the terrace of a Tuscan villa. Look for her cat Toulouse in "Astrodog."

 Cathy knits and makes wood carvings. Look for her dog Jack in "Swimming."

BEWARE OF DOG
I'm aware of you.

Henry Holt and Company, LLC, Publishers since 1866
115 West 18th Street, New York, New York 10011
www.henryholt.com
Henry Holt is a registered trademark of Henry Holt and Company, LLC
Text copyright © 2002 by Amy E. Sklansky
Illustrations copyright © 2002 by Karla Firehammer, Karen Dismukes,
Sandy Koeser, and Cathy McQuitty. All rights reserved.
Distributed in Canada by H. B. Fenn and Company Ltd.
Library of Congress Cataloging-in-Publication Data
Sklansky, Amy E. From the doghouse: poems to chew on /
by Amy E. Sklansky; illustrated by Karla Firehammer [et al.].
Summary: A collection of dog poems, illustrated with beaded art.
1. Dogs——Juvenile poetry. 2. Children's poetry, American.
[1. Dogs——Poetry. 2. American poetry.] I. Firehammer, Karla, ill. II. Title.
PS3619.K58 F76 2002   811'.54——dc21   2001003973
ISBN 0-8050-6673-X / First Edition——2002 / Designed by Donna Mark
Printed in the United States of America on acid-free paper.
10 9 8 7 6 5 4 3 2 1

Artwork contributions by: Karla Firehammer——cover, pp. 10, 11, 28–29, 34, 35,
36–37, 38–39; Karen Dismukes——title page, pp. 12–13, 16, 17, 20–21, 22–23,
back cover; Sandy Koeser——contents page, pp. 14–15, 18–19, 24, 25, 32–33, 42, 43;
Cathy McQuitty——pp. 8–9, 26–27, 30, 31, 40–41, 45, end pages.

The artists beaded on canvas to create
the illustrations for this book.